False Offering

What People Are Saying

False Offering is equal parts rage and rebellion. Mookerjee deftly traces the outrage of a brown femme body in a world where 'white space would always be looming behind,' where she chooses to be a 'gilded thistle,' where her 'ashes will glitter, residue in a dragon's wake.' A rambunctious and important debut that everyone should read.

—SJ Sindu, *Blue-Skinned Gods*

Though an intoxicating mix of "nectar and venom" makes it great fun to watch her take down the false gods of American exceptionalism, Rita Mookerjee's main business is praise. "Stand aside," she commands, "for my/people, my ancestors, and our contributions to the world." Rooted in love of the South Asian diaspora, this powerhouse debut documents what it takes to resist assimilation, survive white spaces, and confront Infidels for Trump. "A combination of/lunar brute force and angelic grace," these poems weaponize style and slay their enemies.

—Brian Teare, *Doomstead Days*

Rita Mookerjee's *False Offering* is a bad bitch, is a heathen's hearth, is a sexy romp through selfhood and lineage, is venom breaking apart the fuckery of empire and white supremacy. These visceral poems are ripe with rage and glittering ashes, "residue in a dragon's wake." They howl for kinship, for ancestral care, and ask: how can we find safety in this world? Full of Sailor Moon odes, tanka trios for Center City, and biomythologies, *False Offering* is "marked for chaos," and I have a kink for chaos.

—Jane Wong, *How Not to be Afraid of Everything*

False Offering

Rita Mookerjee

JACKLEG PRESS

JackLeg Press
www.jacklegpress.org

ISBN: 978-1956907049

Library of Congress Control Number: 2023933888

Cover art by Danielle Taphanel
Author photo by Betty Ann Hill

Contents

For my sister, Trina—
There will be a time when you
will read this in wellness and joy.

i. Little Omens

Let Me Be a Cloth Doll

1.

To begin, cut clean muslin. Keep her in a pot of chai for a few days.
Match my color and my smell. Add two stitches of silk thread per eye.
    Stuff her full of Iowa cornsilk, blacken the tips with soot from
    Pennsylvania coal fires, then briefly press a boysenberry where
    my sour mouth would purse, a favorite snack from childhood
    picked from plants that warned with elegant thorns. Leave
    her nude and place her high on a bookshelf where my doll can
    observe conflict—something my living body cannot do.

2.

I was born right after midnight on a date marked for chaos.
Kindred, make my doll sit still. Naturally, she will crane her neck to the side
    or toss herself from the shelf without warning. In this case, turn her on
    her head to sedate her. It will take time. In life, my serpent temper
    is my essence so when I am calm, people feel ill at ease because a still
    adder is simply digesting or maybe planning who she wants to eat next.
    And I eat so much. After two weeks with her, you should start the burning.
    Speak about narcissism before you kiss her with the match. The cornsilk
    and roasting chai should smell rather pleasant—an incense of release.

3.

Notice how she is so small yet unbearably willful. Aggressive for an inanimate
object, scenting the things around her in smug silence, making the shelf her altar.
    Kindred, I've been bad. Heed my footsteps in this lesson, avoid liquor, do not
    be fooled by slow burns, softness, or bits of cardamom. When you burn up
    my doll, please bind her with a narrow strip of paper that reads *hearts of gold*
    are quick to fold. Know that one day, you will take her outside and in effigy,
    burn her atop oak leaves as they curl. Don't worry about the moon or perfect
    circles. In this ritual, I come apart, but I will try to burn for you with grace.

Common Era

In the 7th century, the astronomer Brahmagupta pauses
his sky cartography and considers some numbers. After-

he writes theories of debt, of wealth, and of a new number.
He calls it zero and is the first to arrive at this idea since zero

is not often a feature of this world, with its excess and bounty
and surplus. Zero was not apparent to the Greeks or the Romans

with their little nude boys, bronze bulls, and virgin brides. All
these amounts of things and time. But because of Brahmagupta,

I can imagine a system of time that starts with the year zero,
a system that isn't punctuated with war or conquest, I can imagine

a way to name this planet and its people in several places, with
several beginnings, but mostly without that baby god god baby

that the zealots often misquote. Everyone knows the baby god's
name as well as the white man they keep him inside, you know the one,

that hunky Anglo wet dream: blue eyes, bloody body, muscled and raw
Even today, centuries later, it is still the year of their lord. They have

kept their monopoly on time and peddled that white homunculus
to every corner of the globe. Let him stand aside as I look for my

people, my ancestors, and our contributions to the world. I am no
child of Brahmagupta, but I see past painted idols and glass kings.

In 1991, Your Letter Predicts the Future

though I never met you

                  or my other grandfather

though I think I would like you more

                  based upon

          the July letter that I now read, though you wrote it

to my mother who you call Chinni   meaning sugar

or sweetheart. Because, Nana, everything you write
is measured, like your advice to my mom on cows
and feeding them as recommended in the Vedas
though I doubt she could find tamarind, jackfruit,

and neem, American cows probably settle for ryegrass
and plain hay. I imagine more greenery in Rajasthan,
and double the roaming cattle, though I see plenty here
in Iowa which is acceptably green, but questionably flat

as though herds seeking sweet corn pummeled the hills
from the ground. I'm not one for the outdoors anyway.
You anticipate this. Your mention of books is uncanny
how you tell my mom to consult with a librarian,

then bring me tales of Rama and Jesus Christ
and St. Francis of Assisi communing with animals.
You recommend hardcover with lush illustrations
so that I too may learn grace and respect for nature.

Did you know, Nana, that I would become
a recluse, only leaving my cave apartment
to buy booze and fresh-cut lilies that shudder
in the heat and scatter neon pollen on my table?

I'm not happy in one place for long, but you understand.
You call Pilani a rather rotten hell for booklovers,

and so I hope that you have wound up somewhere
in the archives, not in repose, but busied with tomes.

In Diaspora

In my town, white families burst and spread
like ripe fruit, ribbons of pulp trailing seeds behind
them while I search in the past for a scrap of skin,
any hints about all these brown people I never met.

I leave the grocery store after not finding
rosewater and star anise and walk home alone.
While I search for spices and a niche that can hold
my odd body, I call up dead ancestors who haven't

the slightest idea who I am   *wrong number*
they say. They hang up and go back to drinking mango
lassi. Which is just as well since we are strangers
but sometimes, it feels like they were never

really here to begin with. In truth, I don't know half
of their names. Maybe they are as real for me
as I was for them. I feel like I could disappear in a mass
of people as a smudge of broken color marks the death
of my family name. Who am I to the ocean that drowns me?

If I Could Rename My Town, I'd Call It Lost

It was something like Dorothy in reverse, clicking my heels
in quiet desperation, willing myself to an emerald city

because the place where I grew up is cursed. Just look at what
sits next to every school. Mine hugged a dog food factory

that reeked in the rain, another straddled the sewage treatment
plant, the third shared land with an asylum. If that isn't enough,

just turn on the local news: arson   arson   kidnap   kidnap
meth lab explodes in the back of a daycare center   more arson.

One kid from my grade became a volunteer fireman so that
he could put out his own blazes and impress his girlfriend.

And that's not even the worst story I know. At least two
dozen people from my class are dead. Mostly from opioids,

some wild accidents like when a guy shot his twin brother
instead of the squirrel he scoped from his window. I don't

recall these plagues of drugs, but growing up, we had active
KKK, flash floods, fistfights, and black ice. You'd never know

you were in Pennsylvania based on the number of Confederate
flags on doors and cars. Some say this was bounty hunter country,

which I believe based on the number of trap doors and secret stairs
in the oldest houses in town, traces of the Underground Railroad

that made the hair on my arms spike up each time my friend turned
a hidden knob, her flashlight daring me up a spindly drop ladder.

Even the county fair gave me the chills with its bloated pumpkins,
toothless lurkers, and an old-timey freakshow that I never braved

firsthand. I used to see the small-town charm, that country beauty
of cabbage butterflies, of flaky birch bark, of old mountains,

of the ears of white corn nicknamed butter sugar sold at roadside
farmer's markets. Then, the Susquehanna surged into the park

and took the playground with it. The flood coaxed cottages
from their foundations, and at last I could see how the town

was poisoned, riddled with rot you can smell in hard apples
and black walnuts that drop onto lawns to expose their dirty,

latticed innards. In the summer, some glassy-eyed deer traipse
into my mother's garden to snap sunflowers off their stalks.

They head to the forest, a graveyard of green spines in their wake.
I see fewer trees now, more dead kids, and double the smoking

guns. I rarely leave the house when I'm home for Christmas,
afraid of what I'll see along roadsides or in icy rain gutters.

One county over, coal fires hiss underground, burning since 1962,
and every so often, a sinkhole breathes steam and brimstone

from a singed belly. On windy days, the air is whipped with ash
and pine. It mixes with skunk spray, a scent so thick and familiar

that it doesn't smell bad at all to my nose. It only serves to remind
me of the truth: that there's no place as bleak or as haunting as home.

Hamsapaksha, or the Swan's Wing Mudra

After days spent being ogled and answering quietly to
butchered versions of my name, I retreat to a thicket
by my childhood home where I climb inside a grey swan
claiming its body as my own. Sticking my neck out, I
stretch my spine until my face is framed beneath
inky lore and a broad tangerine bill. Gliding, I match

wing tips to my fingers and hold them in place like
I'm dancing Bharatanatyam and for a short while
I can be both: a brown girl and a grey swan, proud
and preening. Know this: I am no hunter, just a tiny
thief of affect and skin because in spite of musky pelts,
those jagged quills, I can move through the world

feeling weightless in this way. My prize is the blessing
of repose. But in the end, only one skin is mine. The pelt
grows soggy and putrifies and in this unbecoming,
I am the opposite of Saraswati: not atop the swan
in queenly grace but buoyant with rot below until
the cape of down slides from my shoulders, leaving

me dark, nude, abject. Deep in my pool of swans, I
whisper to the goddess that I am approaching a point
of fracture: a day when I lose this softness and safety
and face the violence of being spotted outright. For now
I'll wear these animals and gold idols and runic charms
because the skin I call my own is streaked with danger.

Each of my beauty marks kiss the crosshairs of someone
who craves the chance to throttle, then shoot me at point
blank range. I cannot escape this truth, so instead I tend
to my downy cygnets, the other brown girls who hide
in plain sight beneath wings and beaks. I keep my fear
on hand, but someday soon, there will be enough of us

to make a legion of brown chimera swan girls who will
take to the skies and upon those hateful masses, descend.

Unholy

This is a myth about red root vixens
maenads and wolves in
a contest to see whose
teeth and claws are longest
trampling damp earth
the rhythmic thudding
of orgasm the violence
of a beak shredding fruit
this might seem like strange
company to keep but if not
wolves then who? They are
honest in their savagery
in their shaggy coats
which remind me that
the body is just something
full to slip away from, that
my jaw locked from forgetting
prayer can open with a scrape
of stone and spill its bait.

Infestation

In the woods near my childhood home, gauzy nests sprawl across
oak branches. I avoid looking at them. They seem like
sloppy webs from afar, but I know that spiders do not

make sloppy things—they choose windows, iron gates,
or spaces between hollyhocks to hang their lace, catching
mosquitoes and patching the holes with darning needles but

their skillful sewing does not resemble the span of white mesh
which shrouds the old trees. My father tells me caterpillar hordes
build the sticky tents, one inside of the other.

From within, they eat leaves padding the web walls against
chickadees and wasps. They eat and work until their
metropolis overtakes the treeline and I imagine

webs floating down to the lawn, braided with shorn grass so
the caterpillars could expand their nests to cover
my house with my family and me trapped inside.

I now know that this was a warning, an early indication that even
if I turned my head and looked away, white space
would always be looming right behind me.

Coconut Oil

As a teen, I wish I knew I had perfect skin
and spent less time shaving my thighs
and the small of my back, rubbing brown sugar
and extra virgin into my feet and arms while
my mom shouted at me to stop wasting water.

I didn't want to peel the brown away, but I hoped
for something more dazzling underneath, maybe
gold or amber? I lived a life far from beaches
so coconuts were rarely on my mind, but once
I anointed myself with clear paste, boys would sit
by me at lunch, a girl at ballet would tell me I
smelled good, and so my oilwork became routine.

My vanity grew loaded with oils. All of them
impart a different slick: some to lure people
in with a dark sheen, some to melt yesterday's
kohl from my lid, some to prime me for escape.
At night, I'd stroke my shins and knead the petals
of my arches. After months in sun on hot grass
and driveways, I saw myself reflected in storefronts
and car windows and decided I would become
a bronze idol, a gilded thistle, a living ember searing
through my hair and clothes. Because of my oilwork
I keep jars all around the house—in the bathroom,
the kitchen, at my bedside—so I always remember how
I coaxed myself from the shower and out into the day.

Nemesis

People admire a sense of industry / a spirited
sort of communism / how the labyrinth
tenants toil away over early blooms / tufted legs
weighted with sundust / convening in their planet
in service of the one true queen / everyone
admires their golden down / but wasps are paper
makers in fitted jackets / ignoring pollen / soaring
missiles / audacious enough to crave human food
is there anything more insidious / than a Jurassic
soldier / choosing prey for food / prey for hosts
/ turning a corpse into a comfortable nest / furious
darts in the fig tree stabbing as many times as they
can muster / nectar and venom alive in one body.

Truly

How can you not be a lesbian when you watched movies with characters named
truly scrumptious / I mean she is on a beach in white frills like a three-layer cake
singing about her name singing about the taste of her / but it's very chaste I mean
I'll start over / you can learn a lot about my sexuality if you watch chitty chitty bang
bang / I don't remember the whole story but there is a faraway kingdom
and a malfunctioning car and a pair of children / but I just wanted to see / truly
scrumptious you're truly truly scrumptious and she really is / because it's 1909
and she is out on the town / cruising in her weird car / precursor to a bad bitch
ruffles on her breasts / she almost runs over those extraneous children / and ends
up all wet in a pond / takes the children to their single father / he is hustling her
trying to sell her on these little / candy tubes toot sweets he calls them / but really all
his sugar flute does is interrupt the movie / every time truly goes out she ends up all
wet in the pond / you're supposed to be happy / when they're on the lam and hiding
from an evil baron who wants truly's stupid car / so everyone hides in a toy shop
and acts like dolls / turn of the century marionettes that abruptly / perform a song
and dance which shows / how in love they are / which shows that the children will
have a mother / when really the most important things are truly's dresses / wisps
of cloud / and a big hat topped with pink roses / another just swirls of white lace / I
wondered if truly smelled like lily of the valley / or exhaust from her car if she
would let me lie on her big dress / and put my hand in her hat

I Grew Eyes at the Nape of My Neck

from spending too much time in white
space which alternates between cradling
me and squeezing my guts out and some
time ago, I reached back and felt them

there, blinking under my dark ponytail.
When I don't use them, they crust with
lymph and old skin. I have to rub
to coax them out of my tendons, knotted

and taut. Open, my eyes all itch as though
the air around me is forever spiked with
goldenrod, and for this reason, I cannot
process comfort: a place where my odd body

ends and the world begins. Eyes three and
four don't react much to light, but they water
in lust, squint at intimacy, bulge at rejection.
They narrow each time that someone deems

me an alien. A problem. An anomaly. A bitch.
In white space, my body shrinks because I
can never extend my limbs to fit the shape
assigned to me. I wish that all four eyes

had powers like heirloom amulets: two
lookouts always on high alert for temptation
and fraud, and two to guide me from niche
to temporary niche until the day comes that

space has been made for my odd brown body
so that I can rest all four eyes and expand to fill
my space. Sometimes I profit from my many
eyes, however swollen, however sore. In white

space, people line up to gawk at the back
of my neck. They nod together to appreciate
my vitriol and scorn. They buy my books, then
rip me from any niche I try to claim as mine.

This Is Not A Form of Play

The Mayas sought your tails for fertility
queer paws tipped in pink cones
country drifter city crawler lover of corners
                    your hiss your teeth
                    you are not brash

you skirt the wayward raccoon
you are far smarter than people who
build house after house   ripping beds from   floors from   walls
you shroud yourself in neglected pockets
leaving labor to rabbits and lesser beings
digging would be a waste of your skill
                    you can recall your favorite meals
                    and lead yourself to corn fields
                    to apples to onions you are
                    cautious when thieving eggs
                    each   dull   diamond in the straw
the moon in a rosy hand
wander far, possum, leave the farm before daybreak
life is easier when you
keep to yourself and you have done the best job
your fainting your rigidity
the elegant clench of your curled spine
                                this is   not a form of play
play is a luxury afforded to those who daywalk
play is the pastime of the aggressor no
all of your acts have a function
each performance curated for some dire purpose
                    the froth   between   your teeth
                    like the surge of high tide
                    come to persuade
                    those who linger

I often see you on roadsides
                    sidesplit   in the margins   red matter

[15]

still I find you lucky
enjoying night as it was meant to be enjoyed
sharing the wise palate of the pig
sparing yourself no delicacy
thriving in places where people forget to look
people forget so much.

Sphinx

On "A Subtlety, or the Marvelous Sugar Baby." Sculpture by Kara Walker, 2014.

A sugar sphinx lies
on her stomach the balls
of her knees pressed
hard into the ground
palms of feet kissing
like this so everyone can see
everything and you don't try
to look away You plan to add
her to your collection. Memorize
the pull of her calves, something
twisted in the way she sits like that,
like it's her natural pose. You cannot
get past the glow between her legs
coming jagged and insistent a buzz
from within a venus flytrap. You long
to prick her with a needle and see what
comes out. Maybe a syrup, muddy and hot
something you could smell underneath
your fingernails all day and night, but from
hours in the light, the sphinx starts to melt
and you will notice the way that she is wet
all over and while you'd love to bite her,
you'd rather watch her auto-cannibalize.

Appeal to Erzulie Yeux Rouge

Don't expect miracles: the grudge
must be true and the offenses
evident. Seek misdirection.
Erzulie Yeux Rouge doesn't
play by mortal rules.
Coat nails in red lacquer.
Light twelve pillar candles.
Carve your enemies' initials
in triplicate at the base.
Fill a glass bowl with salt-
water and three dried chili
peppers. You can use fresh
ones if the grudge is too.
Channel the praying mantis
fire ants all things wild and
livid. See a face both bloodless
and incensed within the bowl.
At 3:00 AM, stir with cinnamon
bark, do your best not to speak.
Pour the saltwater around your
doorstep before you break the skin
of the peppers and release
their delicate fever. Bury each
one because Erzulie Yeux Rouge
walks barefoot in fine soil.
If you are without a yard,
find a park or a potted plant.
She will rise through dirt
and leave her red trail
in the path of those
who have wronged you.

False Offering

Sometimes I look at my altar, all the brass, lavender, and candles, and I worry
that it is too crowded, that some gods can't see their sigils, that the clutter will

confuse the divine. But some gods find beauty in chaos, some enjoy excess like
Thoth. His temples were filled with animal mummies sold by priests standing

along the way to the necropolis. There were mummies of cats, dogs, and crocodiles.
You could even buy a scarab beetle wrapped taut so it lay flat like a coin. The most

belovèd animal mummy was the ibis, white-plumed emblem of Thoth himself.
The ibis was anointed with pine resin, feathers pressed with beeswax. Bowing

the dark scythe of beak to breast, the ibis was folded and bound in linen. Many
people bought the mummy birds to offer to Thoth, but this pattern inspired greed.

False priests bent lizards, coiled snakes, and wrapped these hollow shapes in linen,
dyed ochre and streaked black with tar. Tightly swaddled, no one could see these

chimaera mummies with their faux beaks fashioned from spine. No one except
for Thoth who scoffed and flung a curse at those who falsely worshipped which

made sure their descendants would never know true sleep, would never rest
like the ibis mummy, folded and serene. Standing at my altar, I do not have

a mummy for Thoth, no scarab beetle, no ibis in linen. I don't know if I will ever
have offerings fit for gods, but I'd rather offer nothing than be caught as a fraud.

ii. Demiprayers

Song of the Oyster Girl, Naked in The New World

When I change the thickness of my eyeliner
or tug on my top to lengthen my cleavage
I remember Kitty West who, in 1945, came barrelhousing
out of two shells to delight everyone in the French Quarter.

She'd lie in wait with her arms around a gigantic pearl
and then emerge in a veil making the birth
of Venus look like a schoolgirl waiting for the bus.
She'd cradle her pearl against her cheek

like it was the most precious thing in the world and slide into a split.
With a gilded foot, she'd draw a figure 8 which is the sexiest number
as long as you have a dirty mind and you had to be dirty,
I mean really dirty, to take your striptease out of the clubs

and onto Bourbon Street because anyone can strip well in the dark
there's no challenge in that. A true seductress is a topless daywalker
and you couldn't miss Kitty, though there were a lot of girls
giving the people what they needed in long gloves and sequined pasties

but Kitty took her sexy and mixed it with freaky and came up
with waves of green hair to let the people know that
she was a wayward sea goddess whose top fell off on her way
out of the Atlantic, a savage mermaid

outside of the Absinthe House where patrons sipped
juleps for $1.25 a head. Now I live the legacy of the oyster girl
because these streets are teeming with sex, tits and teeth are not
enough to get what I want; I stay kinky and crazy and bold

and one day my hands will also fill with pearls,
so keep your eyes on your wallet
I'm here to take your money and your man.

Kintsugi

you don't get ears like mine by playing
it safe with silver & cubic zirconia
glittery little lies—no I can spot the real
thing across a room and that fake shit

because at some point women stopped loving
gold to covet its cheaper sisters. I hear people
say there's no such thing as rose gold which
isn't true at all because sure it's made in a lab

but alloying gold with copper and palladium
isn't imitation it's innovation. Who doesn't love
a rosy glow the blush of cheeks in wind a lip bitten
after saying the wrong thing lips bitten while doing

the deed rosy lids fluttering in orgasm. Of course
rose gold is a thing it's a hybrid but you wouldn't
understand that so play it safe in your sterling silver
world I'll be a molten goddess lit from vulva to neck

in the brightest yellow gold dreaming of my lobes
stretched 3 times their size double pendulums
weighted with orbs and facets not a sliver of helix
unadorned two fabergé seashells glinting evil

in the night people can't decide whether to cringe
or to stare the gross decadence of it all: the split flesh
filled with sun because in kintsugi, you take broken
pottery and pipe gold into its cracks: it still looks broken

but being broken in gold is better than being whole
in the first place. In my ears I lock my future adding
a puncture spilling chi for each victory giving new
meaning to the word outshine because these

babies are my bank vault my dragon's den impaling
intruders who dare tread inside no room left for teeth
or bones and I don't pack my ears like this in a doomsday
sense; my gold-hoarding is lusty but never desperate

[24]

nothing like the rows of WE BUY GOLD   shops
lining the shadier streets of any given city the abrupt
command a violent promise of cash. I'd die before I
gave up my gold these loops and clusters are how

a brown girl gets medals for bravery and trophies
for conquest. The value appreciates over time
and I'm not talking about bars and bricks in a yard glowing
underfoot that's what I call a waste it shines because

it was never meant to live in the ground and neither was I
so maybe someone can melt all my jewelry down and grind
it to a fine dust. My ashes will glitter: residue in a dragon's wake.

Ode to the Sailor Moon Transformation Sequence

To catch the anime block on TV, I would rush
home from 1st grade. I would clench my fists
the bus driver took too long turning onto Cherry
Hill Road because there were new villains—like

a half plant, half woman with vine arms, obscene
and flailing but what I wanted to see most was
Serena's transformation sequence, the apparition
of costume-like battle armor meeting ballet.

To follow along, I took a chopstick and painted it pink
tied a hair ribbon to its end. I'd pirouette and arabesque
with my makeshift wand, though the chopstick, unjeweled
and wooden, left something to be desired.

I decided that this was what religion looked like.
It starts in her fingernails. Serena shouts
something and her nails glitter with power.
Then a crystal brooch shoots satin ribbons

all around her body, which is without curves
but still a little sexy in silhouette. At the time,
sexy wasn't of interest to me. I was onto something
cosmic, something in the particles of light flecking

the air around Serena, making her look saintlike
in her silence while her dress takes shape.
Her eyes closed, her lashes fanned out across
her cheeks. The bodice ribbons shimmer

to become a Japanese schoolgirl uniform.
I understand now why this looks so nautical, why
she is a sailor, because the Japanese loved the clothes
of royal French youth sailing with their families

in the 19th century which would later prove to be quite
a formative time for both fashion and fetish culture.
Here in 1996, Serena's hands wear long white gloves,
the ripple of her skirt shines blue as she tosses

her hair back; she's almost dressed. This might just be why
I like to dress slowly. My mom would scream that school
wasn't for fashion, that I needed to eat breakfast, that I
was going to miss the bus if I didn't choose an outfit

but I wanted my skirt to ripple and my earrings
to light up to show that I too was ready to
battle my enemies with a combination of
lunar brute force and angelic grace.

I abandoned the second part, but 23 years later,
I still dress slowly, stroking my dresses, stacking
three or four rings on one finger. They don't
turn into weapons but they look pretty cool.

Two opals at the top gleam pink and green against
my skin. Though Serena wears a choker, I keep it subtle
with my favorite goddesses on yellow gold chains.
I wait for one to speak to me from my throat; she never does.

Tanka Trio for the Inside of My Mouth

An apple keeps its
bones clustered in dense flesh, so
it's strange to think of
the red pulp in my teeth which
I feel in times of fatigue.

No faerie wants these
dented relics wreathed in blood.
Though they're rarely used
for good, I grip them tightly
and wake up with a bruised tongue.

In dreams, I sharpen
them on flint and slate, rattling
their cores. Sometimes they
chip; I suck on the fragments
and hope they find their way back.

Tanka Trio for Center City

I scrape a tangle
of dark hair with a boar brush
between my breasts a
silver pendant swings heavy
and cool: the ouroboros.

Philadelphia
leaves me to bad habits and
the pulsing ache of
a still limb that fell asleep;
an orgasm in reverse.

I prowl the bar at
XIX; the wide balcony
hums and I look for
more bad habits while my rings
swell tight between my knuckles.

Tanka Trio for the Drought's End

I drink Black Russians
all night for a new twist on
bad behavior. Skin
flakes swim in my lip gloss so
I chew them off while I wait.

Only when I've cut
my mouth on too much sugar
do I crave water—
unnatural habit that I
make no effort to correct.

From the balcony
I hold a glass to the rain.
A beggar, I crane
my neck to try and measure
the taut braid of passing cloud.

Kink

You enter a hot trance in the bath mulling
over the occult   jotting notes
        in a makeshift grimoire
                to figure out   100 ways to make
                        your nipples show through your shirt
                dreaming up the right combination of sick
        and sweet open thighs and clenched jaws
                dreaming of a dark bookstore full of
        crystal quartz and rugs for nude lounging
                full of dirty revelations where a dark-haired
                woman intuits what you need
        so that you can focus on glass and girth
    you only keep these habits
if like the sphinx you hold all questions and answers
        so you well up with cleverness and
        hold your codex between your legs.

Ode to Chiapas Amber and the Hands That Find It

I rub my thumb over new plugs
enjoying their slick sheen, ready to stretch
my earlobes to double-zero so I can wear
these amber discs. It's strange to imagine

their origin because beyond the mines,
the people of Simojovel wait while the highland
trunks are bathed in floodwater and their syrup
ebbs into the mud. The resin breathes slow and clear

through the sweetgum like frozen ambrosia
trapping beetles and lacewings in webs
of ancient matter. This is when the people come
with picks and spades, scraping through silt

and darkness. Their hands fissure
in rings around their knuckles,
honing those honeyed geodes full of
wings and blood and scales, those eyes

of god, those stones lusted after by conquistadors
who are immortalized for their goldlust,
but were also entranced by this amber gloss,
so they trapped it in rosaries and rings,

trapped these sap fragments of fell trees that somehow
still swell in earthy pockets and woody slivers.
In Chiapas, men sift through loam while children in old Nikes
rake away the excess and women ferry the barrels

out from the mines. This sweat wins them
a handful of coins, not enough for tamales.
Though the amber is extracted,
cleaned, and buffed, it remains a paradox:

disobedient and yielding, both soft and savage,
with the wildness of some million years. It brings
with it a cycle of transmutation, so even the most
tender pendants, gilded and silverworked,

will yield their amber in beads of sun,
melting to coat something new in its cling.

Fetish/Recluse

I took nighttime to hide in my hair and
considered how I confused lust with
a periscope. How intimacy was a seeing eye,
people's faces in orgasm.

Through muscle memory, I learned to grab a bottle
from thin air. Since it only takes 21 days to make a habit
I hammered this magic in like ideology,
fists unsure what to make of sleep.

I dreamt of fifths of whiskey with false bottoms
filled with index cards listing coping mechanisms
that I could call my own so I could stop
living as a caricature of myself.

Then sleeping alone started to feel like a victory
because I could pass out with wine in my mouth
a lump of gleaming brie on my nightstand
and for all my social inclinations, my time

in bed alone increased. I read the news and
considered myself lucky. I tucked corks into
jars around the house: awards for effective self-
medication. Smug quotidian trophies.

Portrait of Sujata Who Never Dresses Down

In the '90s, I'd roll my eyes as my mom dressed for running errands.
The white moms all favored casual simplicity: old marathon t-shirts

run for the diamonds, straight hair back in scrunchies, denim overalls,
tennis shoes. My mom slid five bangles onto each arm, affixed silver

dangles to each ear, wore long floral dresses that whispered of saris
hanging like bold flags in her closet. She'd need my help with the clasp

on her necklace but never with the tube of lipstick gleaming garnet
in its metal casing and I don't ask, but I suspect that she has practiced

this ritual for ages. I picture my mom dressed up, even as a young immigrant
in the '80s, babysitting for twenty-five cents an hour while my dad studied

diagrams of the heart. They came here with two suitcases and forty bucks,
and I picture her only bag packed neatly with pastel silk skirts, blouses

with pearly buttons, sandalwood shards, and brass figures of gods
she hoped would still be listening in Wisconsin. Decades pass before

I understand my mom's dressing ceremony, this crafting of elegant self.
Though everyone says celebrities go out in sweats and baseball caps,

chunky sunglasses shielding their brows, that is a practice best left
to the privileged. Dressing down is not an option for those

who make housewives clutch their purses, pushing strollers fast,
who are openly stared at from the bank to the mall to the post office,

whose accents make teachers' eyebrows knit together in question,
who wince when TSA agents rake through our hair with gloved hands,

whose uttered language earns scowls at the grocery store,
murmurs of   *how did they all get here?*

To this day, I've never seen my mom in jeans. As a teen in India,
the only place to score Levi's was the black market, so good denim

was mostly out of the question and instead, my mom sewed billowy
dresses in violet and crimson, did her hair in big curls, and piled on

silver that somehow never snagged as she potted basil and chives
and flipped roti on the stove. These dresses and earrings became

an extension of her body, catching eyes in the parking lot
when she picked me up from school, catching breeze on the hill

of our herb garden, catching light and tossing it back to dazzle
those who question her place in a country that is, unmistakably, hers.

I Date God for a While/It's Just Okay

because he likes it when I ask about
his writing, though I read his book,
with its rocks and seeds and fires.
I didn't find it very good.
I tell him about the gemstones in an orange,
about speaking subalterns, red tide, and the deep web;

he praises me for my observation skills.
Each night, I try to remember the universe
as he has shown it to me, but I'm distracted by
white cheese and sweet wine. I tell him about my
research; when I recount his wars, I
ask if he regrets any. He smirks and says   *would you?*

After a couple drinks, he laughs about
Mesopotamia and tells me where to find the
third cradle of man. Like I care. Cradled men
never served me well. When I don't heed
his convictions, he calls me sassy
because mortality is his kink and

he gets off on picturing me becoming
naked becoming bone becoming sand
becoming fiber in the light. He explains
how he'd take me against his thumb
and press me to a star. He gets annoyed
when I ask about the muses or the fates.

He claims there's more to life than loving dead girls.
I break it off when I see him without his mask,
when he thinks I'm sleeping. With his head to the side
I see that he is vapor, sort of a milky smear
I see that it was posture and good lighting all along.
He doesn't kiss me goodbye. I think better of him.

Curio Cabinet

The best curators in the world   are life-takers,
the big ones, like Kamsa   who sought to kill

                   baby Krishna whose parents
                   switched him with a farmer's
                   newborn but everyone remembers
                   Hercules and talks up Moses

        even though it was Krishna who took
        to his godly body best, parting not just one
        but all the seas and killing scores
        of shadowy beasts.
        I read these stories because I am attached
        to my skin and do my best to study
        those who are known to collect bodies though

I don't understand what Hades and Kamsa
do with bundles of 99 souls and all the leftover
mortal shells. *Things are getting pretty crowded.*

On the Death of My Tamagotchi

I was drawn to its translucence
like the gummies I sucked
before ballet. Circuits and wires
exposed through a jellied sheen.
I pried mine from plastic jaws

a reward for perfect spelling tests
plus the bonus word that week:
oviparous. The slight weight of the
Tamagotchi in my palm was
a watery taste of maternity.

With the battery inserted, a handful of pixels
greeted the day. The Tamagotchi with its joyful
head bobs swayed in a modest dance broken
by stillness indicating hunger;
cheerfully flailing with a digital cherry.

I was a benevolent parent until I left
for school. In my absence, the Tamagotchi
poisoned by its own filth, slowly died
leaving me with nothing but a grey corpse
no words just simulated putrefaction.

I begged my mother to take away
the tiny egg to hide my shame high in her closet
but this wasn't enough to wipe the
Tamagotchi from my mind: its double-X
eyes and a congregation of flies

flickering in judgment. My inaction at seven
upset the balance and the universe left me
feeling accountable. This is how I found myself
capable of great violence; how I began as a lifetaker.

Snake Den Haze

I'm never honest about how much I sleep
       but it would be easy to figure out since I turn up
       with smudged makeup, eyes retraced, speckled
       with mascara crumbs. I oversleep a lot. In bed
       I twist onto myself like a red ouroboros,
       aching, stretching impossibly.

I'm always dreaming of snakes and shibari,
       coiling my wishes as I sleep. By day, I am swollen
       and thirsty over well-timed glances or cancelled
       plans because inside of me is a nymph, a hissing
       hatchling who urges me to drink, to slide in and out
       of dresses for people—much like a paper doll—

instead of opening books and washing dishes.
       I'm getting worse at telling people how my day was,
       because day isn't when things happen for me.
       I'd rather tell them about my dream of end times,
       the movie that caused it, or my cervical orgasms,
       but that kind of manic oversharing puts people off.

Cardboard Cutout Palm Tree

While you're horizontal on canvas furniture that
doesn't look the way it did in the catalog, slick can in hand
cold condensation, you're supposed to say *this is the*
life when really you should be asking *is this my life*

because at what point do muscled cabana boys and
flower-tending boys and cocktail-serving boys
become one tan, tropical amalgam, interchangeable
at each location, and everyone wears that goddamn print,

the hibiscus with its showy pistil jutting out like a penis
like a magic wand pointing you to the sample area
where they're offering piña colada espresso shots
appealing to your desire to stockpile mini umbrellas

and antioxidants because these are the things that
you prioritize in Florida. You gulp the shot, and
think that it's the pick me up you've been missing
but when you brew it at home, the stuff tastes like mud

and baby powder, so you toss the whole cannister
in the garbage and open the floral encyclopedia
that hurts your wrists to hold.
you look up hibiscus anatomy, stupid fucking

flower that it is, and you wonder why people don't
favor the pitcher plant or nightshade or gloxinia,
which you read is a greenhouse plant so it isn't
in the nursery with its paved trails painted green

in a bad impression of grass, sprinkled with retired people
who realized too late that they didn't have any hobbies.

Biomythography

You go to that place near the forsythia
and the lilacs, not far from the oak tree
cut down for fear that it would cleave
the house. You walk through the floralscape

before working to shed your body each
evening, shins rattling with growing pains.
The skin on both feet cracked at the toes
mimicking the dead oak. With each échappé,

you opened yourself to a room rank with rosin
and sweat. You whispered chants for salvation,
chants for satisfaction—your small hollows insisted.

You tried to console yourself with stolen tantric
books aged gold and soft, with racy photos in
the bottom of a shoebox. You twisted your torso

across a bed that felt too small. Your body
revealed its allegiance in heat-seeking
to become a chamber of hisses, a vessel igniting.

I Dream of a Goodbye Feast With My Ex

but not goodbye like a breakup, goodbye as in
12-hour time difference, as in holidays together
and nothing else, as in my family in the States
and his in Taichung. The dinner is fun, all
things considered, though only two people
at the table share a language, but translation
is rapid and small words illicit laughter:
crowded   busy   tasty   cheers
The lazy susan spins, my lips coated, sesame slick.
I look at my mom, who is hopeful for me,
who loves my ex like a son and taught him to
pluck meat from his plate with fingers wrapped
in chapathi. I had to teach him to raise his voice
when talking to her, how the constant sizzle of oil
in the kitchen made it hard for her to hear, even
if she wasn't cooking. When I wake up, all these
good smells—fermented tofu, chapathis, kebabs—
are gone and there's only sweat and saliva.
Nauseous, I stressclean my bathroom
pouring bleach into my toilet and scrubbing
until wet flecks splatter my black tank
leaving peach lesions in their stead.
I do not change my sheets; sleeping in sweat
is penance for indulging the dream
as in. This indulgence will stay
on my mind. The memory of this dinner will
spoil my appetite on every date for five years to come.

iii. Heathen Vices

You're Not a Martyr If You're Having a Good Time

From two rattan chairs, I observe my bare house:
the velvet couch, watercolor goldfish,
the vintage table with someone's social
security number etched through the stain,

grim decadence, a cruel canvas for a
six-course daydream while the rest of my peers
fly to Iceland, eat butterfish, and hand-
pick lavender for sock drawer sachets. Packs

of dry noodles that line my pantry say
this ascetic thing looks good on you so
I drown them in soy broth, perch a gold yolk
atop the mass and eat alone on the couch.

There Are Problems in the God Factory

and I know this because I can't hear
anything over the clatter of dead kid bones.
The god planners sweep them up to grind
into meal or paste to bolster the factory walls
then fumble with hot clay, dropping
foul-mouthed half-golems across America
who stomp and spin to distract everyone
from filthy water in Flint and caged babies
at the border. The planners shrug, the country
is rotten anyway. To the tune of prayer, the golems
spear the dead and roast away the soured flesh.
At night, the planners roll up the blueprints
and the tracing paper, delicate as mothwing.
The golems will crack soon and mix with
bonedust. Meanwhile, I light agarbatti
and hide behind digital banshee queens.
because each glance at the news makes
my jaw clench. My teeth chip as my body
serrates its edges. The planners don't notice.
They look to their records for inspiration.
Sekhmet? Kali? Mars? Old Testament?
There's no shame in returning to the classics,
so they open a cask of sea-water wine
and draw up some new prototypes.

About Indian Hair

I.

My father insists that as Sikhs, we should not have haircuts.
My sister doesn't get one until she is six.
Though I mock the cape that covers
her back and frizzes in the rain,

I secretly prefer her curls to mine.
In the sunlight, her hair has
a red sheen like Coca-Cola.
It lies in ringlets near her ears and temples

so I steal a snippet of it when she is busied
with dolls and hide it in a silk-lined box
that holds a marble replica of the Taj Mahal.
It sits like a new tier atop the tiny onion dome.

II.

My mother says the sight of my uncleaned
hairbrush makes her want to vomit,
that it is my duty to pull the soiled silk
through the teeth and into the trash.

After she has scraped my hair high onto the ball
of my skull, she ponytails it, sprays the curls with water,
adds a big ribbon to hide the elastic.
My sister gets a braid ending in a perfect spiral.

III.

I don't find it strange that my mother
does my hair until I sleep over at a friend's and realize
that I do not know how to manage these sopping locks
For some reason, that ritual has been kept from me.

IV.

On TV, I watch the wigmakers rake
raw hair across an apparatus
that looks like a torture device:
a block of wood full of raised needles

while somewhere in Gujarat, deep in a temple garden
girls wait to make offerings from long braids not knowing
that the inky twists will be swept up and sewn into
wefts / weaves / wigs for faraway women to claim and lay.

From the temple floor, they take scraps and strip away the spiky refuse.
I can't help but feel a wet yank on my scalp
while I watch the wigmakers work the hair hard and fast across the tools.
I wonder how there is any left when they finish.

Later, some reporters walk deep into a jungle
to meet a woman who is growing her hair
to sell. She needs to buy food for her family.
She smiles wide and says that giving up her hair will make her very sad.

Rooh Afzah

I tore a rose from its perch
and thumbed its velvet
with plans to watch its corpse
unravel on a table. I readied
myself for the cold trace
of the florist's. Instead,
I smelled Rooh Afzah, that syrup
my dad stirred into iced milk
in the summer, turning the banal
into something pink and singular
in the smallest juice glass
which made the drink sacred.
I never drink milk now.
No stores in this city
sell Rooh Afzah, and most days,
I can't even find a bouquet
of real roses, the kind
I smelled in Mumbai
that made me want to suck
the buds and press the petals
to my wrists to make their scent
my own. I have three dozen
perfumes, and none of them
get it right. I've learned to
expect nothing of shrubs,
boutonnieres, and centerpieces.
Those roses are sterile, scrubbed
of wildness, stand-ins for
the real thing which is why,
just outside my window, I am
shocked to find that honeyed
scent; to be 13 again, tasting
Rooh Afzah on the back
of a stirring spoon.

Marketplace Savant

I want to meet someone who can explain to me
the schools of thought on how to choose a durian,
then tell me which one is best. Someone who can
spot the correct shade of stony lime pearl armor,
who can tell me if the innards will be spongy
or threadlike with white fibers trailing from each

pulpy segment, someone who can knock along
the spine and gauge the level of custard in the flesh,
who sniffs for the irregular sweetness of cream
and onion or butter and almond or garlic
and vanilla and picks the right one on the first try.

Daith

The daith piercing is named after
the Hebrew word for knowledge which is what
its creator needed to puncture the ridge
of tissue disappearing into the canal
tucking a gleaming ring inside.
Most people make it rhyme with *faith*
but really it's pronounced like *moth*
and you'll never know what pressure is
until you've felt this;
the hollow needle threads impossibly
into a part of you, a softened bone
that mostly goes untouched, one that
has an ancient story and a ritual role
and recently doctors have urged those
with migraines to go out and get this
piercing, that it will cure their pain
that this tissue marks an important point
on the head. They say this with confidence
that this sham acupuncture can mend people
and they bring up Eastern healing, so it's a win-win;
if it works it's a new medical innovation,
if it fails it's a relic of a primitive culture folk magic
and it's only a matter of time before
doctors start charging by the thousand
sorry insurance won't cover this new procedure.
They will dig into the soft canal not with knowledge
but with a piercing gun which was only ever
meant to tag cattle and when the placebo
takes hold, patients will thank doctors.

In Spite of My Lavender

I'm never lucky enough
to experience an upright jolt
around 5:00 AM when the sky
suggests light, milky and nauseating.
I take my time falling asleep
because to enter a series of underwater
cities is to consider myself one of
the dead. The caves beneath this
island have nothing for me, and opiates
won't spare me any suffering.

There are patterns I will now transcribe:
lost on a train, teeth scooped from pulp,
death by a thousand cuts, the stranger who
soundlessly moves closer and closer to my
house. The faceless of people in my dreams
makes them feel avant garde, makes me
feel as though I am always experiencing
high art, even when I'm awake.

I keep people in my bed as counterweights.
I hope that they don't notice how I drop
in altitude, untethered by the charms
around my headboard. They have no idea
how much I am putting them to work.
For nights alone, I pump lavender
fog into my room and singe my throat
with tinctures and joints, but I'll still be
flung from a tower or found wading in bloodied
water. My body oversleeps, steadfast like
a magnet. Tomorrow, I'll be late for everything.

Venus As A Demon

After I said I didn't mind
I hid in the nightviolets
watching the new lovers in clairvoyant
silence. My teeth threatened to
popcorn out of my gums.

> *I take pride*
> *in being*
> *easily incensed.*

I considered how Cleopatra
who was not Egyptian
had servants mash a cucumber
with honey and slather it
in a spiral across her back.
they'd leave with filmy
palms: a shared aphrodisiac.
Cleopatra didn't mind this
act of charity because
the water of the cucumber
would dry in a sugared
crust and her consorts would
find her naked and wreathed in bees.

> *that intuition*
> *that self-assuredness*
> *comes with being an outsider*
> *summoning bees and snakes:*
> *the best way to keep*
> *kissing cadavers*
> *out of my house.*

Origami In Lieu of Klonopin

I crease my paranoia into dying stars
people write their wishes on paper
I can't leave them that way
they'll just become lines on my face

in all of this folding my cursed town
swims to the front of my mind
its rows of artillery its collapsing roofs
a gentle burning: all celestial horrors

I seal these memories away in each pentagram
because the past only reminds me of
the many places I can never revisit
how the roads broke when threatened with exits

how my body is a thing to be modified
the way monarch butterflies
cover a deer carcass at the roadside
scarlet wing points ablaze.

Lesson from the Oracle Who Had Seen Too Much

for R.J.

For a time, my professor Regina was one of the lost
women trudging up and down Broad Street. You've
seen the type: an ageless person in a black down coat
too hot for the present weather. The type that prays
out loud to lost gods for a fix or even just a lemonade.
The type that screams as if waking from a nightmare.
The type you avoid eye contact with on the subway.
Regina kept pace during the day and slept in houses of sex

and crack after dark. But past the broken bottles and plastic
cups, up the rotted stairs soured with piss and butane,
she laid in dank rooms and thought of greater things. She
considered the pyramids and how they aligned beneath
the stars. She scrawled prayers to Tehuti on gum wrappers
and dropped them in fountains across the city. She channeled
Queen Nzinga leading her troops to battle the Portuguese.
She dreamt of James Brown onstage camel walking, euphoric.

Regina and the Broad Street walkers saw Philadelphia
grow wicked: scores of cops leering on side streets, cuffing
panhandlers, pulling out batons to bust protestor knees.
All this before the bombing of the house on Osage Street.
In her fury, with time, Regina found like minds. They wore
leather and rolled their hair with wax. But for all the big guns,
raised fists, and dreads, the Panthers were a brotherhood, not
a coven, and she still had many questions hanging in the air.

Regina stays in that broken city as a protector, a keeper
of stories light and dark. She won't talk to cops, but the media is
the specter she hates the most. She once told me in a voice like
bent steel never to watch the news before bed, that it leaves foul
residue in the mind. Leaning close, she said *do not take that filth
with you into the dream world. If you do, it will live in your body
and grow like a sickness.* Though I do my best to listen, with or
without the news, poison swims in my mind all day and all night.

Beach Ghosts

They come in and out of vision
tripping on foam and white dust;
I'm getting used to this kind of mirage
in the daytime with my mouth hot and full of beer

squinting at strangers while beach ghosts
keep pace with a salt rinse
chuckling at the undertow.
This makes me wonder how my uncle drowned:

were his ankles over his ears off the side of a boat
pulled like a swath of hair frothy and tangled,
or was he treading water when a cupped hand
became a closed fist and carried him off?

I picture it in the daytime.
I try to make sense of this word;
it sounds like something that only happens at night,
but I felt that weightless tug around my ankles

one morning when I lost my footing in the pool.
I was spotted quickly by a classmate with strong
hands but the dip of my leg as its strength was spent
sent a dull hum to my fingers,

splayed and pruned. I dared to recreate
this feeling in the bath with a prism
glinting above me, but I was safe against the
tub floor. When my eyes get sea-soaked

and my ears are plugged with water,
I can hear the buzz of the
beach ghosts clearly. They tell me that
there's nothing as haunting as the summertime.

Hard Water

My sister thinks people follow her,
so my parents take her to a ward where
her roommate is a hornet. At lunch,
a man frowns into the payphone
for ages, shakes my father's hand
and invites him to the CIA.
No one is young, everyone is white.
Most of the women are there to detox.
I wonder who comes to collect them
when they check out. The place is loud.

A book, stuffed animals, and lip balm:
the totems on my sister's nightstand
are all I think of now, 1000 miles away from her.

I learn that the water is hard,
and makes her skin flake
at the scalp for weeks.
On the phone, she sounds parched,
and I remember her voice, high
and breathless when we'd get
offstage from The Nutcracker,
how I'd squeeze the warm orb
of her shoulder and reapply her
lipstick for photos. We'd eat fruit
in the car after and doze off,
chatting. Now I wonder if
she gets any sleep at all.

In a luckless turn,
my sister's arms and legs inflate
with fluid and slog at her sides
as she rolls onto the bed.
It's probably from the lithium.
I send her packages of weed
and body lotion, the latter

a flimsy comfort. I daydream
of our midnight snacks,
mimosas and brie, and pray at gods-to-be
to fling this curse on someone else, please.

A Man Threatens to Shoot Me on Behalf of 'Infidels for Trump'

Infidels for Trump reminds me of the Aryan Brotherhood
but I guess the latter is worse. The paradox is obvious

but this is the problem with people who don't read books.
Now don't get on me about class issues and freedom of speech.

You know what freedom looks like? The library where unlike my house,
everyone is welcome. He should have taken advantage of that.

Here's a tip: when you turn to talk shit to a brown chick in a bar,
make sure you're not speaking her language. I mean literally,

speaking her language because while you talk about Aryan
Arya is a Sanskrit word that means exalted which is the last thing

that white people were if we look at technology, advancement,
and dental hygiene. The real irony is that it was my people

who came down from the Caucasus Mountains. The swastika
is the symbol of my goddess, the one who wears a belt

of severed male heads. My people invented numbers and bathing.
The characters in your holy scripture looked just like me

which I know isn't a problem for the Infidel for Trump and it's that
classic redneck confidence that is beautiful. A complete alliance

to the most flawed ideals, deep love for a flag that looks so much like
the Union Jack it borders on adorable. And so I fold my glasses and say

to the meathead decked out in red: I don't know if you know this,
but you lost. You lost and you continue to lose. You rep those colors

in Florida, a notorious traitor state, where men hid
in the salt plants, sunk into swamp mud, jumped to the gulf

and tried to swim to Mexico rather than suffer Robert E. Lee's bullshit
never mind the couple thousand that said fuck it and joined the Union troops?

And don't get me started on Donny boy because those jokes write themselves
and unlike you, I'm no fucking cliché so read a book then come through

and see me sometime, big boy. A black cat will laugh in the doorway
when you drop your PF-9 once I go to work on those Infidel knees

because you people always have the same two problems: no book learning
and a total lack of imagination which is why you won't expect

my Louisville slugger: the icon of a favorite pastime
and I don't mean baseball because I'm not America

I'm not Southern I'm a brown girl and a violent bitch and a loud cunt
my only hobbies are breaking necks and smashing kneecaps

so when you come through be ready to give me that good head
and I don't mean get ready to eat this good pussy you'll never be so blessed

what I mean is watch your neck because
I've got plenty of room on my belt for you.

Love Song for Sourness, Stink, and My Acid Tongue

In college, my girlfriends learned that drinking
vinegar could cure UTIs. They tried the remedy.

I watched them cringe and suffer, but honestly,
that apple cider sting got me the wettest I've

ever been and even now I watch people
wince at raw onion, when—left to my own

devices—I could crunch a red one whole.
What else is a rude ass bitch supposed to eat?

When others smell skunk, I smell luxe onyx
pelts, peaty with white dabs of crème fraiche

and maybe I'm obsessed with dirty, but
not like urea bursting from stone corners

in Union Square. Never the subway or other
people's trash full of plastic and vinyl. Petrol

is as close as I can get. As a teen, I huffed
acetone which was a lot like early masturbation:

flits of good heat when I got it right. Now, I
can take a lemon or a lime and with my teeth,

tear right into the bulb. At first, it hurt to feed
my acid tongue, the skin in my cheeks grew loose

and white with ulcers. But now it is thick and hard
so I can speak to the poetry of swamps; the densest

smells and the deepest pigments: the divine green
gifts in decay. And maybe this is my superpower, so

that when the water runs putrid or foul powder fills
the air, I can brave a bog and run through acid

rain, unburnt, unpoisoned, simply opening my lips to
what stimulates me most; adapting, so fear my bark
and my bite. I am tannin. I am toxin. I am always tart.

Shoes in My House: An Allegory

It's hard for me to tell which of my parents' house rules
are Brahmin and which are just idiosyncratic, but I remember

them all when a friend comes to my place and won't remove
her shoes. My parents' floors stay pristine thanks to my mom

who sees to them every other day and even wipes the dog's paws
when she comes in from the grass so there's no need for bleach.

My parents' floors are always clean, clean enough for the mandala
my mom draws on Diwali in orange and hot pink petals

dotted with chalk and hefty oil lamps filled with ghee,
a precise rune that makes you want to kneel and bow your head,

no matter who your gods might be or how little you talk to them.
The floor is the only canvas big enough for the drawing

and the oil lamps, and sometimes I picture the mandala
in my condo and wonder if I could ever get my floors

mandala-clean. When my friend says she won't
take off her vintage boots, that they took too long to zip,

I recall the white woman on *Sex & The City* shouting
this is an outfit when met with the same request.

Then there was the thinkpiece in the newspaper,
where another broad said *keep your power moves*

to yourself / you don't get to undress me
which floors me, since I can think of no greater power

move than coming to my home and demanding
that I follow your rules, an imperial allegory

so accurate that I almost laugh. When my friend
lets me know she won't remove her boots

I don't tell her about the mandala. I don't explain dirt to her,
how bringing shoes past my door is an affront. I don't tell her

the other rules: how loose hair shouldn't float to the floor or linger
in a brush, that while reading on my bed, when my toes graze

a book, I touch my hand to my head, then to the book to ask
forgiveness. For whatever reason, I keep some rituals and rules

alongside my slabs of ribeye and red wine so really,
I'm no gatekeeper. I don't believe in that mess called caste,

I'm no devotee. Though my feet are clean, my hands are not,
and I know how hypocritical this sounds, how it's typical

of American desis to cherrypick, to extract culture and tout
it with fervor and rage, to honor tradition like a fair-

weather friend. But still. It doesn't change the fact
that I'm the first in my line to smoke and drink,

that I cut my hair and curse, and—more than a few times
—with a weighted bladder, I've dashed through my house

in platform pumps: a warhorse with frantic hooves trying to trample
a made exception. Though I split in contradictions,

when my friend leaves, I kneel to scrub, bathing tiles in bleach
not to whiten but to honor my parents and the ground rules I choose.

On Brown and Yellow College Students Making It Work

Through the Iowa corn fields, I ride the bus. When the international
students get on, I read their Nike, their Supreme to figure out who
has been in the country the longest. They don't need to read me:
The tattoos, the piercings, and the iPhone shoved into a bra cup.

Only American brown girls are this shameless. I smile, but they look off
into the crops. They're not sure what to make of me. White kids always
call them cliquey, but really, they just room together so they can cook
japchae and dosas in peace, without fear of Becky coming in with a wrinkled

nose, giggling to her friends once the bedroom door shuts.
The international students air dry their hair and wear it long, in ponytails
looped low. Although their clothes are taut from the dryer, they'd rather hang
them outside like they do back home. This all makes me think of my parents

living in Madison in the '80s in their studio apartment with the card table,
of the woman who'd pay my mom twenty-five cents an hour to babysit
while my dad studied for comps. Today in Wisconsin, Dorothy's colleagues
have *concerns* about teaching international students. The adjuncts

worry about TOEFL scores, cultural barriers, strange customs
of bows and scarves. I picture Dorothy's hair flip, her perfect
Hong Kong swagger and American scoff combo. She and I have
no patience for this type of talk. As if brown and yellow kids

like us crawl out of straw huts after penning college applications
with sticks dipped in mud, as if half these faculty members could leave
their family behind, fly overseas to end up in the middle of nowhere
with only a backpack, and still graduate top of their class. I think

of the bonds my parents made with other brown and yellow people
in married student housing, pulling all-nighters, just trying to make it work
in a weird new place that offered everything and nothing. In grad school,
I followed suit. I'd eat with Dorothy because our Chinese and Indian palates

fuse together with plenty of slick dumplings, sizzling kebabs, stewed veggies,
and rice to soak up the grease. We'd eat, talk fashion, and make big lesson
plans. I'd tell her how I wish more brown and yellow kids would come
take my classes, learn some radical things, break character, but they're here

[67]

to become engineers, programmers, doctors. I wish they'd come be my students,
because what's more badass than a Pakistani neurosurgeon armed with a gloveful
of feminism, all the fears of white America rolled into one body, slicing through
the breadbasket with a scalpel. I'll keep chasing this vision in Iowa,

where my movers haven't brought my boxes yet, which pisses me off
because all I want are my pots and pans to cook aloo sabzi and coconut
curry, watch the neon splatters color my plates marigold and let the heavy
smell waft through the building to let everyone know that I'm here.

First Day As A Ghost

From atop my headboard, I smell the palo santo I tucked under
the mattress and the agarbatti I lit two nights before I died. I'm

surprised to be able to smell. Of all the senses to keep. My left
finger is still infected from a misaimed knife in the kitchen. It

should have healed, wounds don't suit my hands, elegant like
spiders. I practice introducing myself. Hello. Hell, oh. How do

the dead self-style? Am I still a scholar, just a woman? More
or less divine? I am egg cracked in a bowl, breathless and vibrating.

I push boxes to my Siamese hoping she will bring some books
to people I love. It's no surprise that cats tend to the dead,

at least that much is predictable. At the foot of my bed, no
bhajans or mantras come to mind. Are they spent?

Did I forget? Did everyone? So much for 4000 years
of Vedic theology. I slink off to a bar before I remember

that I have no business there. A ghost walks into the bar.
I wait for the punch line and a whiskey ginger. Am I profound?

Is this a metaphor? A riddle? I wish I could slosh wine down
my front, feel sticky, and blot my skin with a napkin.

Acknowledgments

Thank you to the following publications where these poems or variations thereof initially appeared:

Aaduna, "Coconut Oil" and "Snake Den Haze."

ALOCASIA, "Cardboard Cutout Palm Tree."

The Baltimore Review, "Rooh Afza."

Berfrois, "Kintsugi."

THE BOILER, "Lesson From the Oracle Who Had Seen Too Much."

Dream Noir, Version of "Beach Ghosts" and "Nemesis."

Drunk Monkeys, Version of "Ode to the Sailor Moon Transformation Sequence."

FLAPPERHOUSE, "Fetish/Recluse" and "Kink."

G*MOB, "I Date God For A While/It's Just Okay," version of "On The Death Of My Tamagotchi."

Hobart Pulp, "Common Era."

Indicia, "Portrait of Sujata Who Never Dresses Down."

Juked, "If I Could Rename My Town, I'd Call It Lost" and "Shoes in My House: An Allegory."

Lantern Review, "Hamsapaksha, or the Swan's Wing Mudra."

Lily Poetry Review, "Ode to Chiapas Amber and the Hands That Find It."

Little Patuxent Review, "Truly."

Maudlin House, "In 1991, Your Letter Predicts the Future."

New Orleans Review, "False Offering" and "First Day As a Ghost."

Occulum, Version of "Daith" and "Unholy."

Pigeonholes, "Love Song for Sourness, Stink, and My Acid Tongue."

Pretty Owl Poetry, "In Diaspora."

Pussy Magic, "Infestation" and "Let Me Be a Cloth Doll."

Q/A Poetry, "About Indian Hair" and "Hard Water."

Queen Mob's Teahouse, "Tanka Trio for the Inside of My Mouth" and "Song of the Oyster Girl, Naked in the New World."

Raven Chronicles, "Tanka Trio for Center City."

The Rising Phoenix Review, "Origami in Lieu of Klonopin."

Saranac Review, "Biomythography."

Scoundrel Time, "Sphinx."

Sinister Wisdom, "A Man Threatens to Shoot Me on Behalf of 'Infidels for Trump'" and "Venus as a Demon."

SWWIM Every Day, "I Grew Eyes at the Nape of My Neck."

Sybil Journal, "This Is Not a Form of Play."

The Tampa Review, "In Spite of My Lavender."

Trampset, "There Are Problems in the God Factory."

Underblong, "I Dream of a Goodbye Feast."

JACKLEG PRESS

V. Joshua Adams, Scott Shibuya Brown, Brittney Corrigan, Jessica Cuello, Barbara Cully, Alison Cundiff, Suzanne Frischkorn, Victoria Garza, Reginald Gibbons, D.C. Gonzales-Prieto, Neil de la Flor, Joachim Glage, Caroline Goodwin, Kathryn Kruse, Meagan Lehr, Brigitte Lewis, Jean McGarry, D.K. McCutchen, Jenny Magnus, Rita Mookerjee, Mamie Morgan, Karen Rigby, cin salach, Jo Salas, Maureen Seaton, Kristine Snodgrass, Cornelia Maude Spelman, Peter Stenson, Melissa Studdard, Curious Theatre, Gemini Wahhaj, Megan Weiler, David Wesley Williams

jacklegpress.org

Printed in the USA
CPSIA information can be obtained
at www.ICGtesting.com
LVHW062139211123
764252LV00049B/222